New Smoke

New Smoke

AN ANTHOLOGY OF POEMS INSPIRED BY

Neo Rauch

PAINTINGS

Introduction by John Yau

Poems by Gale Batchelder

Susan Berger-Jones

Judson Evans

Vivian Eyre

Eileen B. Hennessy

Boni Joi

Ronna Lebo

Catherine Shainberg

Marian Brown St. Onge

OFF THE PARK PRESS ○ NEW YORK, NEW YORK

Cover image: *Die Flamme*, 2007
Oil on canvas by Neo Rauch, (German, born 1960)
Painting, 62.99 x 43.31 inches
Courtesy of the David Zwirner Gallery, New York, New York

Design: Shari DeGraw

To contact the press, please write
OFF THE PARK PRESS
73 FIFTH AVENUE, 8B
NEW YORK, NEW YORK 10003

ISBN 978-0-9791495-0-4

Off The Park Press
books are distributed by SPD:
Small Press Distribution
1341 Seventh Street
Berkeley, CA 94710
1-800-869-7553
orders@spdbooks.org www.spdbooks.org

Printed on acid-free paper in the United States of America.

New Smoke

Contents

John Yau

THE POEMS IN THIS anthology came out of a laboratory situation, where every few weeks for the past five years the poets have met to discuss their research. I am the titular head of the group, but I do not direct the conversation.

Mostly, we focus on assignments that might generate writing, which is why we began meeting. The assignment in this case was the exhibition of Neo Rauch's "para" paintings at the Metropolitan Museum of Art, New York (May 22 – October 14, 2007). The reason the group chose Rauch's paintings, beyond the fact that we were all enamored of them, was simple enough; they resisted narrative and did not readily succumb to explication. The figures inhabited landscapes that are unified and divided, seamless and punctuated with tremors and ruptures. Different events occur simultaneously, but they do not seem arbitrary or just another case of that by-now familiar modernist device, montage.

Despite being figurative and seeming to tell a story or at least convey a palpable event, the paintings were not an easy subject for ekphrastic poems, which made them perfect for our research. This was confirmed by the artist's use of a prefix, "para" as the collective title for the exhibition. Did Rauch mean the viewer to think about such states as *paranoia, paradise,* and *paradox*? Did he prefer one reading or did he, as we all quickly concluded, want all readings to come into play? Such clarity is the opposite of ambiguity.

Slipperiness and instability are familiar states which the poet and artist can choose to ignore, preferring a security that is finally false and nostalgic. These poets choose the former, and for that they should be applauded.

Gale Batchelder

Titans

The painting wrapped itself around the tree and commenced framing itself branch by branch, in an effort at reclamation. *Neue Rollen* felt beleaguered by the poets ravaging his inexplicable beauty.

On the other side of the valley, the horses lamented summer. They had heard that in The City you could sit at the bar or sniff around the perfumed room. That season, there was a bumper crop of collars.

In an understandable shift of dimension, the Germans began singing. Music, too, wore uniforms during the days before the fall. Their melodies caused the quiescent landscape to become unruly alligator tendrils, propping up the suit-colored sky.

Thankfully (thought *Neue*), in the fast lane the soccer player crouched by the fallen hands, hoping to eliminate once and for all the yellow. The far peak cushioned the last remnants of smoke, displaying the creed of an earlier time.

Suddenly, data appeared to overwhelm the scene – it was left to diphthong and spectrum to halt them. It was the usual stance, though it could not prevent the limitless shades from a hint of superiority in the game of 'who has more dimensions?'

Everyone agreed, however, to blame this new enterprise on the failures of those responsible for maintaining the theater. In a moment of public bravura, the director exchanged the green pants for feeble explanation, but that did not prevent red.

Their tools were battling for significance, or metaphor, or an ill-described blue.

Painting thought he would never.

Dwell, arrive

I never asked to be drawn lipless,
right hand gesturing a halo,
forsaken by the gilded, parhelic ring.
Here I was materialized:
supplicant to the bearded, muscular chef
and the butcher in red Converse high-tops.
The garnet he-goat, stalwart and rhapsodic,
will lead us to the desert of blue river
neatly crossed by sturdy metal beams
that hint of unsaid sacrifice.
Now place your hand in the open ground
to record the incantations
of the seven stones that lie between us,
because a skull is hardened by the action of the sun.

Isomeric

The whole herd of them incorrectly lumbering over
    monopoly houses.
On a shelf, little winged feet of blown glass

cold as the chunky maiden goddess with Bette Davis hair,
collared and cuffed in topcoat.

One is wearing the lawn like a hula hoop.
The child's spinning top grins its saw-tooth middle,

while past the curtain, the future of Christmas tree has been torn.
The red ladder runs out to catch his pocket.

Who forgives the blue landscape of dry sheaves forlorn at the
    edge,
the lone voluptuous belly posing as a smoke charmer?

The train station diner windows are past reflection
for those lurking, cross-hatched by un named shade

in the underground of the dead soldier imprisoned by
    turquoise.
We have blackened one wing of the angel amputee.

While the subsidiary argument brought on by the orange-
    shirted men,
quavering and quivering in the deepest green,

and the assistant slashed the flaming yellow answer:

A diatomic molecule in which the nuclei have opposite spin
directions.

Martin Luther Revises His Theses

1. Napoleon is sharing a beer with Holmes, who hasn't a clue as to when the Boy Scout scarf flew in and tried to strangle Dr. Freud
   a. There still is cause for wonder
   b. The dream of finally claiming it

2. The uncharted death wish collapsed like a card trick

3. So you've got a little tic and a penchant for waving peanut flags
   a. Really, it's fine to draw attention
   b. A trough of low pressure

4. If you don't watch out that origami ceiling is going to smear your jelly
   a. Remember that form follows excitement

5. Already I see the smoke of years piling up
   a. (I never really wanted all that anyway)

6. The dotted tendrils cut clear through and have you noticed I hoisted my ticket between your legs?
   a. Desire severs longing

7. Don't look down at me in your double breasted misery (oops, did I say breast?): but I wasn't marking us
   a. They say the Madonna statue shed tears
   b. The right to claim it.

8. Isaac Newton stopped by lest we forget *gravitas*, but his gray-matter face is obscured by the lapse
    a. In our world, bodies dive crow-like from towers, shadow puppets against smoky skies

9. His palest third arm grabbed an ego swatter and he's threatening the little man
    a. Because he knows that deduction is the new divinity
    b. Accept the shining ransom

10. I think there's a shooting star erupting the hat
    a. Even if it's just one, forlorn. Still.

11. Why are we crowded in one corner getting all the attention while George Washington is in the library chanting hieroglyphics?
    a. There is no space in modern art
    b. It was a time of low rents and withheld ambitions

12. Running pointedly to blue when the red shirt wore the pants
    a. The color of regret is yellow

13. No excuse for doing yoga with a paintbrush, especially when a mirror
    a. Delusion seemed the key to survival

14. That mother looks kindly at the little village being masticated by the furry trunk
    a. Nothing left from the windmills and rockets
    b. Against the will of fate

15. I see it's already got an aura but the three sturdy students are applauding
    a. There never was a reason to wait for a sign

Susan Berger-Jones

Crust Topiary Of Alms: A Primer of Pool Tables

o o o

Safe from larks, the crusty paths with cows are better ware wolf watching spots. Unless milked, pilgrims may be unescorted by stars or snow. This is the only range where the Golden Ducks can lie down. By noon a last farmer loosens a pound of fairies and they bitch. Under raging clouds, children struggle with the grass and rub rude lambs. Otherwise the ridges of an Armada sing out Armistice, as denoted by Industrialists still on vacation. (And look at all of those Elephants in the Caravansary!)

o o o

Where are the windmills? No one recommends nap time as it is too humid to pose or twist. When the Posse comes to town, the children aim their petty-coats in a yearly star gazing event that leaves the town coated with velour. So as not to disturb them, we are as soft as werewolves. We explain why shy swans lay feathers to make sick toys. The townsfolk park Caravansaries. During the next migration of baby blue Chevy's, Christmas tables are filled with girls. (So are the Libraries!)

o o o

Just as angels are fenced in with nudes, Baptismal fonts convert windmills into struggling vacations by May. The Elephants have not been painted and the wedding threatens snow over the range. Many have become rudely lamb-like as the tracks of stars are bleating for licorice. A group that gathers for Kaddish wish that the late locomotives would arrive with those new boys!

o o o

Golden ducks lay divas in the snow without cows which are now safe to eat in Europe. Admiring the sound of backpackers allows tooth fairies to lose a hundred pounds, but no one remembers how warm it was last year even when cobble stones are steamed in porridge. Dumb rented children use the unwritten to kill swans while tied to vacations, wearing pint sized milk cartons gathered for Kaddish, because the loco-motive that speeds here with Golden Ducks is also carrying those new boys! (Hurray! Hurray! Hurray!)

Lullaby

and turn tidy
to yellow ants.
Uniformed jitters play
transparently through rocking socks.
Pogues are hungry for charcoal dunes.
Global darkness comes again some rain.
As a blue tooth eats pork into blue ear disease:
the sky is falling and gray pigeons
shed roses to the grass.
The grass' raked prints
are naked with the moonbeams' antelope and barracks.
Char the ring around your hair in the Posey,
the Posse at noon
is a June in the park.
Your shoulders
are everywhere
weasel among frog ponds,
alms and armies and athlete's feet.
Fungus under the eaves.

The Museum of Forbidden Chalets

The BauHaus is quiet
among the Institutes for Obsessive Diaper Whisperers.

Dobermans are hunted on the Ring Strasse.
A Fraulein picks up Woody Allen asleep in the Black Forest.

Schultz reads his misplaced copy of "Mein Kampf"
encoded with the ID chips of lost kittens.

While following the official directions of torch singers:
"The sun spreads jello over grass' tender rapport."

Understanding the grass is like a slow waltz.
You ladle Gazpacho into the Bunker.

Didn't you know that kittens can conceive of abstract statements?
Didn't you know that every door you see is rain?

Do I think, therefore, I ran?
Did you free the enemy and they are Chalets?

Stoking white snow into yawns,
my sailor pulls assassins from the ponds.

UnColonial Aqua Ringlets

He loves her if she is an envelope. She writes to see ice.
The husbands are walruses, tied up and too tired to work.

The women are pulling buttons off shirts and dropping them
    in the ice cube trays.
The house is a place to watch the Ringling Brothers because it is
    butter free.

Where the huntsmen were once in jail now they are icing the
    porch.
In the Conservatory the rest of the Naval Flotilla sails from the
    jetty to govern the house.

The very thought that a map could be jettisoned lies fallow in
    the farmer's field.
Some are young and plough the field, some sit and wait for
    bottle flies.

The workers complain but an area is cleared ahead.
The hunting party sits where the grass hides the beautiful grouse.

The husbands are haus fraus, too tired to cook pheasant
    under glass.
The women wear beautiful walruses in their trays and hunt
    down Paraguay.

Beware of tilting walls floating among Flotillas as the dens
   govern ice.
Don't iron the house unless the Ringling Brothers are inside
   your brother.

The Flotilla sleeps in a layer of butter.
He loves her nape and envies her plough.

Don't peek through drawn curtains or leave your sandwiches
   to go for a walk.
Don't eat hors d'oeuvres until walruses declare that haus
   fraus live in Oregon.

Drains are clogged by letters when she writes to the Flotilla.
And yet when she hoists up the flag she clogs up Paraguay.

Only a house stands in Paraguay.
She sips mermaids in cups.

He leans too far over the steep frog pond.
She loves him if he is under glass.

He writes letters to the Ringling Brothers.
They are housebound in the snow.

Judson Evans

Fog Mirror

The room in the pop up book can't close.
Too many tabs mash the seams between contestants.

Limbs are tucked into the green felt of pastoral.
Some are maimed, others lost.

A drawer must be left open to err on the side of leniency.
If it seems empty, like clouds seen from a downed airliner,
it is just displacement due to a shift in migration.

Stigmata are invited down with lures.

(This is the film where she teaches a young miner how to read.)

A blind is brought indoors still redolent of musk and unicorn
bed curtains, which folds by the double-jointedness of secret guilds.

The long patience of rites, one finger at a time,
fluorine green where her skirt mosses over.

In her deadpan drill she mimics taking aim,
her shadow puppet of cranes.

She sharpens like an anchor without a test tube of regret.

A man in the plush of his kill can tamp down an older man,
afford him the raking of coals.

(This is the film where the stepson can't prove himself
to the gunslinger step father.)

In an autumn of raised arms, he lights his cigarette with a
      crossbow.

An injured swoop of togas ushers in a soundtrack with a
      Theremin.

The beak is a stylus. The blue-black sheen of a 45.

He constructs weapons from appendages of the body,
causes tools to rust to their vestigial cruelties.

Initiation once supposed the taking of vows.
Now, without a lap dance, he revisits the Old Masters,
invests in taxidermy.

In order that the blue and green cohabit, he must break the code,
cut loose the pendulums.

The air conditioner has been left on since the witch trials,
softening his macho by appoggiatura.

(This is the film where he climbs to the mountaintop,
speaks to the whirlwind.)

The other discovers a downward dimension, an arrested flyway,
frozen computer screen.

Climbing sideways from the daguerreotype,

debriefing the prey, he leaves his shopping list
of prophecy.

New Order

Arguing for an island, a splice
of barrel staves around a moment's
presentation held at arm's length, a city
made of words...

Bridging funds have been cut,
but the closing has been phrased
ambiguously.

You can catch them carrying things out
at all hours. Tickets come with flashlights
and maps, enigmatic as unexploded
ordnance.

A color wheel determines tasks and roles,
the purging of nostalgias
in a voluntary bonfire.

Out of sandblasted stone
it is hard to find *style zero,*
communion at the tabula rasa,

flags, and coins, and costumes,
new prayers and terms of abuse 悯岡
the backward swastikas on Navajo spoons,

or the Hopi rain clouds that reverse
the marathon of ancient Greek key patterns.
Mathematics in the mud, scribbled geometry

     half dry, half erased, each
     catenary clause, each arc
     of interruption,

the beading back of nectar
to the hummingbird s beak

Homunculus

It is hard to love someone attached to your body like a camera,
with ghostly hands, inflated with thought bubbles. The one to beg you
not to crush him, filed like four leaf clover in a book. Many
    dependencies
between the covers those mornings of thunder. The one on top with
    the title
is made of wood. A face works its way through the wooden surface,
    a hummable
argument from one side of the dream. It is free of splinters of the
    door on which
it is painted, but one sided, liable to be locked. Like bats without sonar,
certain clusters before speech form colonies of undifferentiated cells.
History is a matter of scale, or etiquette. A love letter cut from capitals
of headlines. Passing notes, prison mates before the Constitution
    changes
hands, shave off rust together, make toasts with their fists. They
    snuggle up
under the eaves, but it is safe to harm them. They eagerly share a
    blood meal
with those they groom. Their bodies, like votive urns, are purposely
    flawed,
built around evacuation routes that feed the dead. A draft encircling
the birthday cake draws in the fog, each lit candle the beacon
of a lighthouse. They mash out light, spoil it for secreting.
Put floorboards back in place. I feel an upsurge disarrange my wig,
as a flag of uncertain nationality unfurls in the attic.

Vivian Eyre

Paranoia 2

Actors lean into insults from a throb of light.
A script is no defense against yellow.

When I bear down on air,
My hand is a drift anchor.

Degas said: One has to commit to a painting,
The way one commits a crime.

Is it criminal if twisted cords hang from borders?

A doppelganger moored in contemplation.
Kiddy pool with shark fin.

Alice in W's black leather boots
in starting gate position.

Souvenirs: sausages and kebabs.
Two-state alarm for a missing door knob.

File cabinet puffs on electrical cord.
Smoke ghosts a doorway.

Green spills like Neel's Pregnant Betty.
Canvasses forced against a curtain.

I have only a ladder to climb to the ceiling.

In the modern world, there are no windows.
Light is framed and hung from a wall.

Neo-Funghi

My training has taught me a thing about killing:
how dodder seeds leech,
which lethal cocktail for each swarm.

This dome I'm under is no blankety-blank Church.
I'm genuflecting in a patch of spike rush.

Just another day as a boy scout
crouching under a toadstool.

I twist myself into a tourniquet
pray this stipe is toothless.

Whatever lies beyond this field
I can fight it with a match stick
or rifle loaded with neonico.

No one hears the sugar lerp's cry
when he can't stop his honey-machine.

My skin is a million ears.

Wonder if I can stand up under this dress?

Puffballs-Rust mites-Smuts

Eileen B. Hennessy

That *is the dark side of* this:

the side of light speeding

Who started this option? Maybe
the person who backdated the light
to reverse its course, move it
to a new starting gate where the children
could take sides of their own.

The lightness of children falling!
The darkness of children standing
where street and sidewalk meet!

So many years to reach this point.

Which side will the next light take?

Three more miles across the grassy treeless plain

before we start to get close to our markers:
the woodpile and the well, the roadside stand
of the man who sells the knotted kilometer cords,
the quicksand pit. Then three more miles

to the town with the meat market,
the coal market, the sheep-dealers' pens,
the saloon with the violin and the piano
and the men who lean on the bar
and watch the whores dance naked. Then out

and beyond to the miles of wood and water,
fire and metal and earth, always more and more
miles of bearing our body, our mind,
our unknown silent selves.

Boni Joi

Harmless Walk-In Fridge

I chewed the hot pink gumball off my hand
while testing my knife skills

an impenetrable smoke decanted
out of my head filling up the top
half of the window display.

the woman in the cherry hot shorts held a pamphlet of
salmon quizzes.

Square thought bubble really hurt her
the effect was minimal in the balloon light

that was the point when hot shorts decamped and Botticelli
took over.

My chopped oyster mushroom was a given
it looked too much like the merchandise she sweated over

this was uncommon in the bowling alley

the contact of a turquoise shirt
made me pitch wet.

Nexus

Woman wearing babushka window shops
blatant argyle and cobalt bag

roof points toward exploding midday clouds

Bomb or fish?

The lizard walks on uneven skin

tuxedo man leans to proscenium
doll leg kicks out of his lats,

playthings in the window
display of exodus.

Coffee velvet performers stand
perfect pompadours and slate script

chinese characters projected by klieg lights

sovereign disco ball swooshes
leaves a comet's trail,
burnished and smooth like ribbon candy.

The red garbage can brims with firecracker boxes
against a wall connecting all houses.

the bomb pointing toward the people remains ignored

a bomb in the garbage is worth nothing
on the street of a narcoleptic.

Frau Direktorin

Main character: A street lamp
which doubles as Deneuve's makeup,
her attention sapped by the chartreuse umbrella.

Under custom smoke
the Music Man glowing gold
drags a stretched accordion,
he also plays Pepe Le Piu.

Why is she squatting?
That blocking is not in the script
her maroon purse open on the slate
waiting to be crammed.

It's a only a prop!
The audience should believe in the whole costume.

Send in the fried yellow eel with Queen Anne's lace in its mouth.
Can the unidentifiable building come a millimeter closer?

Shoot back to the window
if it rains, can she use that blank expression?

Remember to cut out the sex scene,
or at least separate their hands.

Pepe, who is not the leading man,
loiters as Anemone, Neighbor, Dark Cloud, Neo Rauch and Shrubbery.

Take that melamine out; we are not on a farm!

Can someone please blow up the pink squiggles?

Coming Back Home

Meanwhile, the cult of blue trainers pointed icicles,
a dry-roasted goatee,
three crimson dormers,
seven dark rail station chickens,
a medicinal indigo rag,
the barnyard church steeple,
and a hand in the shape
of a gun forecast in all directions
at the man with carrot lotion and pop jacket.

On his lap, an open briefcase packed with scratch-offs.
Why shouldn't they act vinegary in front of him?

Ronna Lebo

Bluest Elephant

a girl makes green smart-bombs for everyone
with farming, or framing that is time turning the rotunda white
forget the barbeque; it is only there as fire orange afterglow
fill in your blue histrionics with space requirements for reading
    while sitting
on ramps to the Lincoln Memorial
fauns watch a wheel pipe churn the processional
sounds of massive dirt displays by central tractors
marking off the Merovingians with Italian red caps

"Yes," thought Door, "I more or less trust him."

there are fields of what look like Czechoslovakia in the distant
    foreground
behind the Disney sculpture where stage-lit storm clouds billow
    in blocks
of assembly and sharp objects from the furnace room form a hump
that is brilliant but nothing else
adult about keeping it in until it pushes out at the edges
crucified on a large wooden X shape made in communist China
where normally is in the way of being remembered like Confucius
had knocked together several old pallets and a broken gate
through which the world wished to be deceived
with one skinny vertical stripe of cerulean sky everything
    stopped moving

the friars surround us in their hesitation, buckle their shoes
    a monumental phosphorous moment leaks into the only
    reflection in the river
crested from the tale of a grand joke in a carriage coming the
    quicker for it
past posters of gunshot proletariats glued to cement walls
four-color beasts and black-and-white invectives scatter from
    the platform

"Listen, I know what I must look like."

the arrival of parody hasn't made it in time
hard red plastic seats stamp tricky lines along the beach
and the army takes a step towards Us to say We

We escort you away from here and then we let you go.

Konspiration

El Greco built the first cartoon:
white paint as light and heads all in a row
put the brown stripe on Goya's pants
next to a man with a roll of raffle tickets.
Quentin Tarantino fried cheese and corn dogs
or clown gloves after polka...
This painting is a plane window, oh no it's not, it's the light
fixtures on a ceiling fan on a wall instead.
Can these culottes be over soon? especially on that man.
There is the money bag under the table
and a Loch Ness that belongs in Canada.
I am interfering with myself through definitive history.

I said I could do this because it is a story.
Roberta is not in the story, but Raymond Pettibon is,
so are Bunuel and Kentridge, and some Canadians.
Opera is no rarity in South Africa or Germany.
Italy has opted for Cirque du Soleil.
We can ignore Michelangelo; the French are.
Represented outside the salon with the X Men,
the Dutch haven't helped us lately.
I know you are in here because of the smoke.

Sleeper Train

Dwight D. Eisenhower made his speech to the
industrial military organism on the same day
I was just on the point of shimming myself with detail

7 tiny snakeheads poked the pond into squiggles.
Janine wore a ball of air over her head
to build a house underwater, and Vikings arrived in China.

We all read about cyborgs in the holiday manifesto
then put them on the sky next to Cindy Sherman.
What is so easy to understand is Richter's complete
desolation.

I smelled it again;
the bottom of an oven was covered with fiberglass spray.
An apricot lies sweating on the pink table.

White Batman continues to earn every gang
relevant badge to wear at fashion functions.
The tips of his horns will be handy for the sheep dip.

Thereafter, the whistle will complete every sentence.

Job

On Thursday, I was hired to babysit for the Baptists.
I tried to display the underside of a superior therapist,

I flung myself at a handful of prominent thoughts,
I stuck out my tongue in that momentary fashion of the day.
It was a delight to see me there, I wasn't there

if you want to know the truth, I was outside
kissing an unseemly contractor on the foot.

I was engaged in prompt pricing techniques snagged
by a petite chicken in a store window.
Baptists are tough customers and rarely deterred;

their parenting license was last seen affixed to the handset
for decibels measured in a squirrel's screech.

Agency astronauts struggled in the file cabinet next door.

If ever there was a hope, it had been moderated
in the sandlot and auctioned as a trademark,
if we all remember properly.

Catherine Shainberg

Failed Identities

He's a yellow gloved cartoonist
Abstracted from patterns of fossiled cumuli
Good loss of body
A caked over vase lolls in sunken narrative
Here the representation is altogether
Fire in the house   bombs outside
Hieroglyph autumnal sentences
No flag or fiction can wrap around
Heads burn like a woman's minotaur
The predator in the red town thinks, logic
Two men are lemons, two women peck at each other's lip
Her scarlet shoes in a corner lounging towards her
Black winged bed their crumpled latitude

After Neo Rauch

from right to left an unreflective window
like a sadness of dead wings in pine
the locked body of a square phantasmal hall
earth turned inside out, genitalia exposed
its gold unblinking fluorescent drained
life, ascended like antelope horns
despoiled coral, spreads its claustrophobic tentacles
dead bull, caked blood sky
a trinity of wheels lost to each other
miner to miner before a bone filled wheelbarrow
dust to embryo returns
trembling in the latex gloved hands
yellow fingers, child man flopping like a lost bird
over Father's vast trembling chest

Postcard

Last night I was having dinner with J
we were talking about different alternatives
he said: Write to my friend M… and say to him
    Dear M
last night I was having dinner with J
we were talking about alternate realities
he said: Write to my friend M… and say to him
    Dear M
last night I was having dinner with J
we were talking about breaking the limit
he said: Write to my friend M… and say to him
    Dear
butterfly's wings caught in the jam
last night I was having dinner with
we were looking into the mirror
he said: Write to my friend … and say to him
last night we were eating with our mouths
against the wall
we were breathing in a chalky taste

Marion Brown St. Onge

Waiting for the Barbarians

> after Neo Rauch: *Warten auf die Barbaren,*
> Constantine Cavafy: *Αναμονη τους βαρβάρους*

Their husbands are all tied up today.

No more sagging scarlet togas
upbraiding maelstroms,
abolishing pockets.

Baristas, sick of dressing normal,
wound their way through
empty plazas.

Test them for compasses and sensors.
Perform jujitsu moves
on alien colors.

Precocious Rose Beasts see straight
through bricks and cockpits.
Locate Jackalopes.

Put the Pantheons into their places.
Load their guns–then shoot them.

In this Hunter's Room

The air is stale

You can almost smell the men's
clandestine mindscapes

Their drooping shoulder holsters
and pickaxes

The glaucous *pflucker* caught
in the middle

The near absence of blues is electric

A map speaks watery urgencies
but no one notices

Du willst feuer, mein alt es?
The doors yawn

These are no great-blooded outdoorsmen
given to vermilion discussions

Luscious purple moors
Golden Armagnac

Lap dancers

This is an autumnal bunker
going nowhere

What we're looking at is a landscape
of migraines

The weight-bearing beams must have
cancelled thinking

Why else would the hunters ignore
the pretty yellow scribbler

stuck in the corner?

Their friend who's swatting at
the pasted-on dancing ladies?

The blasphemous *schriften* of birds
The swinging to music

After the Fall from the Second Coming

The cardiovascular systems of foster children will blossom
from windfall funding, as will fractal trees
and river systems.

The sky in diamonds will be their bunnies.

Whales – those *grands amateurs de beauté* –
will spout copious tears, making
the waters deeper;

Be happier than they've been in years.

Avatars will have their day. This will please the moon,
for obvious reasons.

Country cottages will find their minnows.

Hospice workers will develop routines so funny
the dying will die laughing at
preposterous jokes.

No longer required to spend their Golden Hours
pointing the way to the end
of the tunnel,

Angels will inspire poets to paint.

Bickering Brothers will make it up; beat
their drumsticks together
under toadstools

Chase mailmen for rubber bands.

Diction-obsessed chicks will drop drawls for boys.

Apollinaire's rabbits will send *calligrammes*
to the *Wall Street Journal*.

Lucifer's helpers will continue to spread their feathers
to the bright indifferent morning
—*bleu comme mon coeur triumphant.*

Too late except for a baby

They are sailing bingo chips and
paper airplanes from the
tops of buildings.

But the water is rising. The sky
is orange. Canaries
are fainting.

Heroes who lifted lines with ropes
up to the 17th floor?
They're gone.

Look! The green's gone, too.
Her diaper is brown.
Thank God.

Though old, I am strong and
I can row. Let me
take the oar

—Get us out beyond the grim
façades and worn out
machinery.

Please! Don't peter out now
—lose yourself and us
in reminiscence.

It will take two to decode the stories
emanating from under
the rubble.

Quick! – I'll take the baby while
you push the boat
from shore.

Jump in now. Here's the baby.
Hold tight.

Heave-ho.

About the Authors

GALE BATCHELDER lives in Cambridge, Massachusetts. She has studied poetry in Provincetown, New York, and Cambridge, with Elizabeth Alexander, Gail Mazur, John Yau, and Tom Daley. Gale has read her poetry at a number of venues in and around Cambridge and is a member of the Concord Poetry Center and Grub Street Writers. An accomplished singer, Gale serves as President of the Mystic Chorale, a community chorus featuring world music. She received her B.A. in philosophy from Beloit College, holds Master's degrees from Boston University and Harvard, and is the founder of New Leadership Group, a consulting firm serving non-profit organizations internationally. The pieces in this volume represent the debut of her poetry in print.

SUSAN BERGER-JONES grew up in a home/art gallery in Pittsburgh, Pennsylvania where her earliest memory is of dancing with a kinetic sculpture. She received her B.A. from Vassar College and her Masters in Architecture from Columbia University. Recently her poems have appeared in "No Exit" magazine.

JUDSON EVANS is Director of Liberal Arts at The Boston Conservatory, where he teaches Ancient Greek culture and literature and a course on Utopian Communities. His work is represented in the third edition of Cor Van Den Heuvel's *The Haiku Anthology* (Norton, 1999), in the first English language anthology of haibun, edited by Bruce Ross: *Journeys to the Interior* (Tuttle, 1998) and in a chapbook *Mortal Coil*, from Leap Press. His poetic monologue *Scrabble Ridge* was staged as a performance piece by choreographer/dancer Julie Ince Thompson as part of the Fleet Boston Celebrity series in 2000. He was chosen as an "emerging poet" for the Association of American Poets by John Yau, and a selection of his poems with an essay on his work by John Yau appeared in *American Poet* in September of 2007.

VIVIAN EYRE'S poems have been published in a variety of literary magazines including: *Spoon River Poetry Review, Poetry Motel* and *RiverSedge*. She has been a finalist for the Dorothy Daniels Award sponsored by the National League of American Pen Women. In 2005, Vivian collaborated with Carolyn Parello, on a series of poems and paintings for the Visible Word at Stevens Institute of Arts & Letters.

EILEEN B. HENNESSY is a native of Long Island, and lives in New York City. Translator of foreign-language documentation, and adjunct associate professor of translation at New York University, her poems and short stories have been published in *Artful Dodge, Cream City Review, The Literary Review, Paris Review, Sanskrit,* and *Western Humanities Review.*

BONI JOI received a M.F.A. in poetry from Columbia University, and has been nominated twice for a Pushcart Prize. Her poems have appeared in *Arbella, Long Shot, Driver's Side Air Bag, Big Hammer, Mind Gorilla, Torch, The Brooklyn Rail* and many other journals. They have also been included in the book *Mortified: Love is a Battlefield* (published in 2008) and performed several times in "Mortified," the acclaimed national show based on the book. A clip of her performance was featured on National Public Radio's This American Life during an interview with the editor, David Nadelberg. She has read her poetry at numerous venues in New York City and elsewhere for the past 17 years.

RONNA LEBO received an M.F.A. from Mason Gross School of the Arts, and currently teaches at Kean University. She performed for twelve years as Alice B. Talkless, won a Jackie 60 "New Artist Award," and was included in two CMJ music festivals. In 2007 she received a New Jersey State Fellowship for the Arts. Her poetry has been published in *Ocular Press*, *Arbella*, *Long Shot Magazine*, *Big Hammer*, *Words*, *This Broken Shore*, *Whim Wit*, and the anthology *Will Work For Peace*, edited by Brett Axel.

CATHERINE SHAINBERG has a M.F.A. in poetry from New York University. She founded The School of Images, a Kabbalah school to advance awareness of imagination as a tool for healing and creativity. Her book *Kabbalah and the Power of Dreaming* was published in 2005. Her next book *DreamBirth* is forthcoming. She has been published in *More Poems*, *Alan Dugan's Poetry Workshops* series, and *Guggenheim Public*. She has been a member of the writer's group, Off the Park, led by John Yau, for the last five years.

MARIAN BROWN ST. ONGE retired in May 2006 from her position as founding Director of the Boston College Center for International Partnerships and Programs. St. Onge received her M.A. and Ph.D. in French Literature from Boston College, where, before becoming CIPP Director in 1991, she coordinated the Intermediate French program, developed new curricula in French business and culture, piloted international internship exchange programs, and directed BC's Women's Studies Program. A former President of the Massachusetts Foreign Language Association, St. Onge has been the recipient of several fellowships and awards from organizations including the National Endowment of Humanities, The Ford Foundation,

Fulbright, the American Association of Teachers of French, the French Government and Sister Cities International. In spring, 2006, she served as Michael Dukakis Visiting Professor in International Affairs at the American College of Thessaloniki, Greece. St. Onge has published travelers' guides, articles on twentieth-century women writers, cultural issues and topics in international education.